A Study Guide

BASED ON THE BOOK

Kay Arthur

Our Covenant GOD

WATERBROOK
PRESS

A Study Guide
to OUR COVENANT GOD
PUBLISHED BY WATERBROOK PRESS
5446 North Academy Boulevard, Suite 200
Colorado Springs, Colorado 80918
A division of Random House, Inc.

Quotations from *Our Covenant God:* © 1999 by Kay Arthur

Scriptures in this book, unless otherwise noted, are from *New American Standard Bible* (NASB), copyright The Lockman Foundation, 1960, 1962, 1963, 1968, 1971, 1973, 1975, 1977. Used by permission, all rights reserved.

ISBN 1-57856-184-1

Copyright © 1999 by WaterBrook Press

All rights reserved. No part of this book may be reproduced or transmitted in any form or by any means, electronic or mechanical, including photocopying, recording, or by any information storage and retrieval system, without permission in writing from the publisher.

Printed in the United States of America
1999—First Edition

10 9 8 7 6 5 4 3 2 1

The Crimson Thread

A companion Bible study to Our Covenant God

- Your overall goal in Lessons 1-4 is to more fully appreciate how the concept of covenant saturates the entirety of Scripture. We will explore what Kay Arthur calls "the crimson thread of covenant woven throughout the fabric of God's truth from Genesis to Revelation."
- Your immediate goal in this first lesson is to become thoroughly familiar with the foundational covenant passages in Genesis (the book of beginnings) and the truths they teach—and to allow God to show you their significance in your life.

Begin your study time by asking for God's guidance to help you learn what He wants you to understand about this wonderful and far-reaching topic of covenant.

1. In Genesis 6, in the account of the Flood in Noah's day, we find the first occurrence in Scripture of the word *covenant,* which in the original Hebrew language of the Old Testament is the word *beriyth.* (You'll find helpful information about this and other biblical covenant terms at the end of this chapter.)

   a. Read Genesis 6:11-21. Which verse in this passage mentions the establishing of a covenant?

b. Who initiated this covenant?

c. With whom did this person establish the covenant?

d. From the evidence in this passage, what appears to be the reason for this covenant?

There it is: God obligating Himself to preserve man in the midst of judgment. Without anything on Noah's part—without any commitment, pledge, or guarantee—God obligated Himself. Do you catch the faint but sweet scent of grace wafting in the wind?

—Kay Arthur in OUR COVENANT GOD, Chapter 3

---

2. The events described in Genesis 9 occurred after the Flood ended and Noah and his family and the animals left the ark. Look carefully at verses 9-17 in this chapter.
   a. How many times do you see the word *covenant* used in these verses?

   b. With whom exactly did God establish this covenant? (List everyone mentioned.)

c. What particular promise did God make in this covenant?

d. How long would this covenant be in existence?

e. What "sign" was given with this covenant?

3. The Bible's next mention of covenant is in Genesis 15—one of the most revealing passages on this topic, as well as a foundation for the rest of Scripture.
   a. Look first at verse 18, which summarizes the entire chapter. It's also the first reference in Scripture to "making covenant." In this verse, who was it that established a covenant?

   b. With whom was this covenant made?

4. Now let's explore the rest of Genesis 15, beginning with the first eight verses.
   a. How would you summarize the concerns on the mind of Abram (later Abraham) as expressed in verses 2-3 and in verse 8?

b. How would you summarize all that God communicated to Abram in verses 1, 4-5, and 7?

c. What do these verses teach or imply about God's commitment to Abram?

5. For further understanding of this covenant, focus your thoughts now on Abram's response as recorded in verse 6. The Hebrew word translated here as "believed" carries the idea of an unqualified commitment of oneself to another.
   a. As indicated in this verse, what was God's response to Abram's belief?

b. Genesis 15:6 is one of the most important verses in the Old Testament, and it's quoted prominently in the New Testament as well. Read Romans 4:3 and 4:18-24. In these verses what does Paul teach as the most important lessons to learn from Abraham's example in Genesis 15:6?

c. Paul also quoted this verse when writing to the church in Galatia. From what he wrote in Galatians 3:6-9, what does Abraham's faith mean for us—how does it apply to Christians today? (Do your best to state the answer in your own words, even if the full meaning of this passage is difficult at first to grasp.)

6. Now let's observe the actual covenant ceremony described in Genesis 15, as we reflect on its deeper meaning.

   a. In verses 9-11, what specific things did Abram do after God instructed him?

   b. What promises and glimpses into the future did God give to Abram in verses 12-16? (Look also at verses 18-21.)

   c. According to verse 17, who or what passed between the pieces of the sacrificed animals?

d. What do you think this represented? (For clues, refer to any of these passages: Exodus 19:18 and 24:17; 1 Kings 18:38; Acts 2:3-4; Revelation 15:8.)

7. Two chapters later, when Abram was ninety years old, God renewed this covenant and extended its meaning. This chapter (Genesis 17) is another foundational passage for understanding covenant and the entire Bible.

a. How many times in this chapter is the word *covenant* used?

b. Look at the covenant command God gave to His partner Abram in verse 1. How would you restate this in your own words?

c. What promises did God make to Abram (who now is given his new name, Abraham) in verses 2-8? List them all.

d. What promises did God make to Sarai (who's new name from God is Sarah) in verses 15-16?

e. What covenant requirement did God give to Abraham in verses 9-14?

f. To whom did God extend the covenant in verses 19 and 21?

g. Summarize Abraham's response as recorded in verses 23-27.

Covenants within human relationships have happened throughout history in cultures all around the world, as H. Clay Trumbull convincingly showed more than a century ago in his landmark book *The Blood Covenant:* "There are historic traces of it, from time immemorial, in every quarter of the globe.... This close and sacred covenant relation, this rite of blood-friendship, this inter-oneness of life by an inter-oneness of blood, shows itself in the primitive East and in the wild and prehistoric West, in the frozen North as in the torrid South. Its traces are everywhere. It is of old, and it is of today; as universal and as full of meaning as life itself."[1]

8. We'll close this lesson with a look at evidence in Genesis of covenants made on the human level. Read each passage below, then record whatever customs or procedures you see mentioned there as part of the process of making covenant. (The word *covenant* [Hebrew: *beriyth*] is rendered as "treaty" in some translations of these passages.)

   a. Abraham's covenant with Abimelech in Genesis 21:22-34.

   b. The covenant between Isaac (Abraham's son) and Abimelech in Genesis 26:25-30.

c. The covenant between Jacob (Abraham's grandson) and Laban (Jacob's father-in-law) in Genesis 31:43-54.

Are you starting to gain a clearer picture of what's involved in this somewhat strange concept of covenant? Lawrence O. Richards writes, "The notion of a covenant is unfamiliar today. But the concept of covenant is utterly basic to our understanding of Scripture. In Old Testament times this complex concept was the foundation of social order and social relations, and it was particularly the foundation for an understanding of humanity's relationship with God."[2]

9. Review the answers you've written in this lesson. What evidence do you see of the solemn, binding nature of covenant?

10. Record what these six words mean personally to you, in your own relationship with Him: *Our God is a covenant God.*

What Exactly Does "Covenant" Mean?

Now that we have started our biblical exploration of covenant, it's good to clarify an important issue: When we see this concept appearing in Scripture, what ideas should come to our minds?

To fully appreciate the meaning of covenant let's look carefully at the specific Hebrew and Greek words used for this concept in Scripture. Together these two basic designations—a Hebrew word in the Old Testament, a Greek word in the New—are used about three hundred times in the Bible.

In the Old Testament

As noted earlier, in the Old Testament the Hebrew word for covenant is *beriyth* (pronounced "ber-eeth"). Notice how scholars have defined this interesting and ancient word: "A compact (...made by passing between pieces of flesh)";[3] *"Between nations...*a treaty, alliance of friendship; *between individuals...*a pledge or agreement;...

between God and man…a covenant accompanied by signs, sacrifices, and a solemn oath that sealed the relationship with promises of blessing for keeping the covenant and curses for breaking it."[4]

The history of this Hebrew word *beriyth* (as scholars piece it together) offers further insight: "The most general opinion is that it is derived from the Hebrew verb *barah,* to cut, and therefore contains a reminder of the ceremony mentioned in Genesis 15:17."[5]

"Cutting" Covenant

Usually in the Old Testament when we read in our English translations about someone "making a covenant," the phrase includes the two Hebrew words *karath* and *beriyth*. The verb *karath* in this expression literally means "to cut off, cut down, fell, cut or make (a covenant or agreement)…. Basically *karat* [or *karath*] means to sever something from something else by cutting it with a blade."[6]

So to "make a covenant" is literally to "cut covenant."

In the New Testament

In the New Testament, the Greek word for covenant is *diatheke* ("dee-ath-ay-kay"), meaning "A disposition…a contract—covenant, testament."[7] "From early times the Greeks used *diatheke* in the sense of a will. In contrast to a *syntheke,* which spelled out terms of a partnership, a *diatheke* permitted an individual to dispose of possessions any way that person chose. The decision, once expressed in a will, could not be annulled by another party. But the will became effective only after the person making it died."[8]

Having looked closer at what the words of covenant mean, let's continue through the pages of Scripture to observe the dramatic stories and profound teaching passages in which these words are used. And we'll remember the big picture as well—that the entire Word of God is itself a Book of Covenant.

THE SECRET OF THE LORD

A companion Bible study to OUR COVENANT GOD

- Your goal in Lesson 2 is to become thoroughly familiar with God's covenant dealings with His chosen people during the time of Moses and to grasp the significance to your own life of the truths taught in these Scriptures.

  Remember to begin your study time with prayer in worshipful and loving submission to your Teacher, the Holy Spirit. Claim for yourself Psalm 25:14—"The secret of the LORD is for those who fear Him, and He will make them know His covenant."

1. As we move in our study to the book of Exodus, the time period is more than four centuries after the days of Abraham, Isaac, and Jacob as described in Genesis. The descendants of these men—the people of Israel—are now slaves. And they are dwelling *not* in the land that was promised to them by God's covenant, but in Egypt.
   a. Read Exodus 2:23-25. In covenant terms, what was God's response to Israel's cry of suffering?

   b. Now look over Exodus 6:1-8, which occurs just before Moses confronts Pharaoh for the first time with God's command to let Israel go.

Summarize what God reminded Moses of and how it relates to covenant.

2. After God delivered and redeemed His people from Egypt "with an outstretched arm and with great judgments" (Exodus 6:6), He met with Moses at Mount Sinai to give His people the Ten Commandments and all the Law.

   a. Read Exodus 19:3-6. What specific promises did God make to the people if they would "keep" His covenant?

   b. In Exodus 34:28, what other term is used to describe the Ten Commandments?

c. How is the Law referred to in Exodus 24:7?

3. Read Exodus 24:3-11, which records a solemn covenant ceremony taking place after the giving of the Law. Summarize here all that took place as part of this ceremony.

4. Let's jump ahead momentarily to the New Testament book of Hebrews, which tells us more about this ceremony in Exodus 24 while teaching us the deeper significance of its meaning.
   a. Read Hebrews 9:18-20. According to this passage, where did Moses apply blood in this ceremony?

   b. The author of Hebrews then considers a later point in Exodus when Moses consecrated the finished tabernacle. Read Hebrews 9:21. Where did Moses apply blood in this situation?

   c. What is the full importance of covenant blood, according to Hebrews 9:22?

5. We now move forward to the end of Leviticus. In this book God teaches His covenant partners about His holiness and about how it must be reflected in the way they worship Him.

   a. Read verses 3 and 9 in Leviticus 26. If His people obeyed Him, what did God promise to do in regard to His covenant?

   b. Now read verses 14-25 in the same chapter. How would you summarize what God promised to do if His covenant partners were not obedient?

   c. Yet even if God's people endured these calamities, God's covenant mercy would still be with them. They could repent and experience His favor. Read verses 40-45. In two different verses in this section, God repeated what He would do in regard to covenant if His people repented. What is it?

6. How would you summarize what you have learned so far about the centrality of covenant in God's relationship with His people?

At Sinai, God also gave exact instructions to His people for building the tabernacle. The tabernacle—much more so than our church buildings today—was the very focal point of the people's relationship with God. Was the tabernacle central to this relationship because *covenant* was so central to the relationship? See what you discover about this below.

7. The innermost part of the tabernacle was called the "Holy of Holies" or the "Most Holy Place." In the very center of this room rested an "ark"—a gold-covered chest of acacia wood, which God had commanded Israel to make. A certain name for this ark is used more than fifty times in Scripture, and we find the first occurrence of that name in

Numbers 10:33, as the ark was being carried away when the people moved on from Mount Sinai. What is the ark called in this verse?

8. So the ark was in the center of the Holy of Holies, which was in the center of the tabernacle, which was at the center of Israel's relationship with God. And inside this ark were the stone tablets on which were written the Ten Commandments. What did Moses repeatedly call these stone tablets in Deuteronomy 9:9-15?

9. Let's briefly jump ahead again. Many centuries after Moses died, Israel's King Solomon built a permanent temple in Jerusalem to replace the tabernacle.
   a. On the day the temple was dedicated, Solomon specifically pointed out what he had put inside it, according to 2 Chronicles 6:10-11. What was it?

   b. Now look at Solomon's prayer of dedication for the temple, which begins in verse 14. In this prayer, what did Solomon say first about God, as it relates to covenant?

10. Now let's jump even farther ahead. Look at Revelation 11:19, part of John's vision of God's eternal heaven. In this passage, what did John see?

11. While the people of Israel were on their way from Sinai to the Promised Land, we read about God making a special covenant with Phinehas, who was the grandson of Moses' brother Aaron. Phinehas was zealous to protect God's honor when immorality and contempt for God were running rampant among God's covenant partners. You can read the story of his bravery and devotion in Numbers 25.
    a. What kind of covenant did God say He was making with Phinehas, according to Numbers 25:12-13?

    b. In verses 11 and 13, what reason did God give for this covenant commitment to Phinehas?

12. Closely related to God's covenant with the priest Phinehas was His covenant with the entire priestly tribe of Levi, whom Moses blessed for being keepers, or guardians, of God's covenant and God's Word (Deuteronomy 33:8-11).

a. What covenant responsibility did God give to Levi in Deuteronomy 10:8?

b. How is God's covenant with Levi described in Malachi 2:4-5?

c. For what does God commend Levi in Malachi 2:6?

d. In this passage the prophet Malachi is relaying God's word of admonition to the priests and Levites of his day. Look carefully at verses 1-2 and 7-9 of this chapter. What were the priests and Levites in Malachi's day doing wrong?

e. And what was God's announced punishment
    for them?

f. Notice in 1 Peter 2:9 what is true about all
    believers in regard to priesthood. What, there-
    fore, are the most important lessons we can
    learn from God's words concerning Levi?

We journey next into the book of Deuteronomy,
where the covenant word *beriyth* is used more often than
anywhere else in the Old Testament.

Deuteronomy means "the second giving of the Law." In
this book God prepared His people for taking possession of
the Promised Land by carefully reminding them—through
His servant Moses—of what He had done for them a generation earlier at Mount Sinai (also called Horeb).

13. For each of the following verses from Deuterono-
    my, summarize the covenant truth Moses wanted
    the people to remember:

a. 4:31

b. 7:9

c. 7:12

d. 8:18

e. 17:2-5

14. How is the content of the book of Deuteronomy described in 29:1?

15. Deuteronomy 29:9-13 clearly and powerfully sum-
    marizes what covenant should mean to God's
    covenant partners. What do you see as the most
    important points mentioned in this passage?

16. As another warning, in Deuteronomy 29:22-25
    God presented a glimpse of the future, a horrifying
    sight that strangers would encounter in Israel.
    a. What would the strangers see (verses 22-23)?

    b. What would the strangers therefore ask (verse 24)?

    c. And what was the correct response to their
       question (verse 25)?

17. Before we move on, let's look at one more especially significant reference to covenant in Deuteronomy. It's an unusual prophecy given by God Himself to His servant Moses. Read the prophecy in Deuteronomy 31:15-20. Summarize the essence of this prophecy as it relates to covenant.

Andrew Murray in *The Two Covenants* points out that here in Deuteronomy 31 we find "a thing without parallel in the history of any religion or religious lawgiver: that Moses most distinctly prophesies their forsaking of God, with the terrible curses and dispersion that would come upon them."[9]

Israel would indeed do the unthinkable: Despite all God's warnings, they would *break covenant!* And because of what covenant is and always will be, there was no possibility of getting around the awful consequences.

18. You're to be commended for persevering in your study to this point. You've processed a great deal of meaningful material. Now in time alone with God, review what you have written down and learned. Perhaps you sense something here that

God wants you to especially understand and trust Him for at this time. If so, go back and mark it in the lesson, then bring it again before the Lord in prayer and grateful praise. Record here any further thoughts or prayer requests that come to your mind and heart.

FROM EVERLASTING
TO EVERLASTING

A companion Bible study to OUR COVENANT GOD

- Your goal in Lesson 3 is to see and to cherish God's covenant faithfulness to His people from the time of Joshua through the time of the Old Testament prophets, despite His people's continued lack of faithfulness.

Once you understand and embrace the reality that God is a God of covenant, you will experience a peace, a strength, a security you have never known. The Word of God will take on a whole new dimension—delighting you with wonder as you explore the height, the depth, the breadth of what it means to be in covenant with God.

—Kay Arthur in OUR COVENANT GOD, Chapter 2

---

1. After Moses was taken home "to lie down with [his] fathers" (Deuteronomy 31:16), God granted the gift of Joshua's godly leadership to His covenant people as they entered the Promised Land. All is well in the book of Joshua until we reach the account in chapter 7 of an Israelite named Achan, whose sin led immediately to Israel's first military disaster. "So the hearts of the people melted and became as water" (verse 5).
   a. Not knowing of Achan's sin, Joshua fell to his face and implored God for an explanation.

What did God say that Israel had done wrong (verses 10-11)?

b. At once God presented Joshua with the procedure (verse 14) for finding out the guilty one. What was to be this person's punishment (verse 15)?

c. What reason was given in verse 15 for such severe discipline?

2. The rest of the book of Joshua chronicles the people's success in conquering the Promised Land. At the end of the book, after Joshua had become "old, advanced in years" (23:1), he brought Israel's elders together to give them a warning. Read his words in 23:14-16.

a. How does Joshua bring honor to God in verses 14-15?

b. What did he say would cause the people to experience God's anger (verse 16)?

3. Soon Joshua summoned Israel's elders once again. On this day he spoke his famous words recorded in Joshua 24:15, "Choose for yourselves today whom you will serve...; but as for me and my house, we will serve the LORD."
   a. Read verses 16-24. How many times did the people verbally commit themselves to "serve the LORD"?

   b. From what you see in these same verses, what did Joshua seem to understand more deeply than the people did—both about God and about themselves?

   c. After their repeated commitment to serve God, how did Joshua respond in verse 25?

d. What did Joshua do next (24:26-27)?

One of the most revealing illustrations in Scripture of covenant commitment is the account of Joshua's dealings with the people of Gibeon.

4. Gibeon was "a great city, like one of the royal cities," and its warriors were all "mighty" (Joshua 10:2).

   a. Nevertheless, the Gibeonites were afraid of Israel. What did their fear prompt them to do, according to Joshua 9:3-6?

   b. In verse 6, what did they request from Joshua and the men of Israel? (Throughout this chapter the word translated as "treaty" in some versions is actually the Hebrew *beriyth*—"covenant.")

5. In Joshua 9:7-8, notice the hesitation of Israel and Joshua to agree to this covenant. How does Deuteronomy 7:1-2 help explain this hesitation?

6. Listen to the Gibeonites tell their story in Joshua 9:9-13.

   a. Which parts were not true?

   b. Observe the response of Israel and Joshua in Joshua 9:14-15. What did they fail to do?

   c. If Israel had asked for God's counsel in this situation, what do you suppose He would have told them?

   d. What did Israel do to confirm the covenant with the Gibeonites, and who took part in this (verse 15)?

   e. Briefly summarize what happened next, according to Joshua 9:16-27.

f. Why did Joshua and the Israelites not destroy the Gibeonites?

7. Joshua 10 tells us of astonishing developments resulting from Israel's covenant with Gibeon.
    a. According to verses 1-6, what caused the trouble in which the Gibeonites found themselves?

    b. How did Joshua and Israel respond to the Gibeonites' request for help (verse 7)?

    c. Now consider carefully the conclusion of the story in verses 8-14. In what ways was God actively involved in this battle?

d. In this situation, why do you think God supported Israel so directly and decisively?

No matter what it costs, a covenant is a covenant is a covenant. Covenant commitment is meant to be unbreakable.

—Kay Arthur in OUR COVENANT GOD, Chapter 8

As we move forward in Scripture, we find a tragic decline in Israel's covenant sensitivity.

8. What happened after Joshua's generation died out (Judges 2:10-13)?

9. In His own perfect faithfulness, God was quick to respond to this covenant violation. What was His response, and His stated reason for that response (Judges 2:20-21)?

We advance now to the time of Israel's kings. In a later lesson we'll explore at length the rich covenant relationship between two brave warriors: Jonathan (the son of Saul, Israel's first king) and David (chosen by God as Israel's second king).

10. Turn to 2 Samuel 5:1-3. By this time David had achieved recognition from all the tribes of Israel as their king. This passage shows him making a covenant (or "compact" [NIV]; the Hebrew word again is *beriyth*) with Israel's elders.

    a. This covenant was made "before" whom?

    b. What action followed the making of the covenant?

11. Later, David brought the ark of the covenant and the tabernacle into his new capital, Jerusalem. "On that day" (1 Chronicles 16:7) he led the people in a special song of thanksgiving. What is the theme of the lines recorded in 1 Chronicles 16:15-18?

12. With Jonathan, David had known the privilege of the strongest of human covenants. But he also

received the even greater honor of a personal covenant from God, in what we now call the Davidic Covenant. Read 1 Chronicles 17:7-14. List here everything that God promised to do for David in this passage.

13. The Lord appeared to David's son Solomon one night after Solomon had finished building the temple. The story is recorded in 2 Chronicles 7. As God spoke to Solomon, how did He refer to His action toward David (verses 17-18)?

14. Now turn to Psalm 89 and look at the following three parts of it. How does God refer each time to His agreement with David?
    a. 89:3-4

    b. 89:28-29

    c. 89:33-36

15. Because of what David knew about the nature of covenant, he could go to his death with calm assurance of God's faithfulness to His promises.

a. "The last words of David" are recorded in 2 Samuel 23. In verse 5, how did David describe what God had done for him?

b. In what ways, if any, do you understand that David's words are true about your life as well?

16. After David's death, Solomon built the temple and praised God for "keeping covenant" (1 Kings 8:23; 2 Chronicles 6:14). But how well did King Solomon himself fulfill his covenant requirements? Let's find out.

a. What does 1 Kings 11:4 say about Solomon?

b. In 11:9, what was God's response to Solomon's behavior?

c. How did God define Solomon's offense in 11:11?

d. What would be the consequences for Solomon's failure, according to verse 11?

17. Solomon had broken covenant and could not avoid the consequences. But what did God tell Solomon in 1 Kings 11:12-13?

The kingdom of Israel, which David had united and passed along to Solomon his son, was split in two after Solomon's death. There now was a northern kingdom called Israel (with the city of Samaria as its capital) alongside the southern kingdom of Judah, where David's descendants remained on the throne in Jerusalem.

Solomon's kingdom was broken—*because covenant was broken.*

But Solomon was not the only leader of Israel to break covenant. And the consequences were even more tragic for those who followed his example.

18. How did the prophet Elijah summarize the sins of the northern kingdom of Israel as he cried out to God in 1 Kings 19:14?

19. Nevertheless, God did not immediately bring an end to the northern kingdom; in fact, He still protected them. What reason is given for this in 2 Kings 13:23?

20. Eventually the same covenant that gave God's protection to Israel would by necessity bring His judgment. What happened to Israel, as recorded in 2 Kings 17:5-6?

21. What reason is stated in 2 King 17:15 for God's judgment of Israel?

22. God's warnings kept coming to the southern kingdom of Judah as well. 2 Chronicles 15 records one

of the rare occasions when the king and the people responded in the way God desired.

   a. Read verses 1-2 of this chapter. What message did God give to Judah's King Asa and the people?

   b. How did they respond, according to verse 8?

   c. Verses 9-14 tell us of a covenant that the people made with God at this time. What actions were involved in the making of this covenant?

   d. How did God respond, according to verse 15?

23. Something similar happened hundreds of years later during the days of King Josiah, when the long-neglected Book of the Law was found while the temple was being repaired. 2 Kings 23 tells the story.

a. What exactly did King Josiah read to the people, according to verse 2?

b. After the reading, what did Josiah and the people do next (verse 3)?

Nevertheless, Judah's days were numbered. Less than fifty years after Josiah led the people in this covenant ceremony with God, Judah was sent into captivity in Babylon. Why? God's prophets made the answer clear.

24. In the passages below, what did God want the people to understand about their sin?
   a. Jeremiah 11:9-10

   b. Jeremiah 22:7-9

   c. Hosea 6:7

   d. Hosea 8:1

25. To escape this approaching judgment, the rulers in Jerusalem tried to "cut a deal" with the powers of darkness, as we read in Isaiah 28:14-19.

   a. What did these rulers boast about (verses 14-15)?

   b. What do you imagine this agreement with darkness might have involved?

   c. How would you summarize God's response (in verses 18-19) to their boasting?

Once covenant is broken and the time for its curses has come, escape is impossible.

Therefore Judah's judgment came about just as it was foretold. She was taken captive into Babylon (2 Kings 25:1-21; 2 Chronicles 36:15-21).

But of course this was not the end of her story. The same prophets who cried out in witness against the people's breaking of the covenant also foretold, in a variety of phrases and pictures and promises, the Lord's inauguration of a New Covenant, as we shall see.

26. In time alone with God, review what you have written down and learned in this lesson. Perhaps you sense something here that God wants you to especially understand and trust Him for at this

time. If so, go back and mark it in the lesson, then bring it again before the Lord in prayer and grateful praise. Record here any further thoughts or prayer requests that come to your mind and heart.

FROM OLD TO NEW

A companion Bible study to OUR COVENANT GOD

- Your goal in Lesson 4 is to become thoroughly familiar with the New Covenant as foretold by the Old Testament prophets and to recognize its fulfillment as taught in the New Testament.

As we continue exploring Old Testament prophetic passages, reflect on their words with a mind and heart open to their message—for they tell of the most important covenant and the most wonderful news in the history of the world…the good news that brings you to God as His child forever.

Ask God to open your heart and mind to begin taking hold of these treasures.

1. Through the prophet Ezekiel, God provided an impassioned and graphic picture of His people breaking covenant. This picture is presented as an allegory in Ezekiel 16. As you read this startling chapter, summarize your answers to each of the following questions to help you gain a glimpse into God's heart and feel how deeply He regards His covenant commitments.

   a. Here in Ezekiel 16, "Jerusalem" is represented first as a newborn girl. What was her condition in verses 4-6?

b. What did God do for her in verses 6-7?

c. After she matured, what did God do for her in verse 8?

d. What did God do for her in verses 9-13?

e. What was her condition in verses 13-14?

f. What did she do in verses 15-21?

g. How would you describe the tone of God's charges against her in verse 22 and in verses 30-34?

h. What punishment did He outline for her in verses 35-41?

i. What emotions come through in God's words in verses 42-43?

j. What summary charge did He make against her in verse 59?

2. Now look at God's surprising words to her in verses 60-63.
   a. What promises did He make?

b. To the best of your understanding, in what ways would God fulfill these promises?

Jeremiah 31:31-34 (reprinted below) includes the first explicit mention in the Bible of a "new covenant." This passage represents the pinnacle of the prophet Jeremiah's words and perhaps of the entire Old Testament. It's also the longest Old Testament passage quoted in its entirety in the New Testament (in Hebrews 8:8-12).

3. Using different colors of pencil, pen, or highlighter, (a) with one color mark every occurrence of the word *covenant* in the passage below; (b) with a second color mark every occurrence of the words *will* or *shall;* (c) with another, circle every name or pronoun referring to God.

JEREMIAH 31:31-34

[31]"Behold, days are coming," declares the LORD, "when I will make a new covenant with the house of Israel and with the house of Judah,

[32]not like the covenant which I made with their fathers in the day I took them by the hand to bring them out of the land of Egypt, My covenant which they broke, although I was a husband to them," declares the LORD.

[33]"But this is the covenant which I will make with the house of Israel after those days," declares the LORD, "I

will put My law within them, and on their heart I will write it; and I will be their God, and they shall be My people.

³⁴"And they shall not teach again, each man his neighbor and each man his brother, saying, 'Know the LORD,' for they shall all know Me, from the least of them to the greatest of them," declares the LORD, "for I will forgive their iniquity, and their sin I will remember no more."

4. Continue your study of this passage by answering the following questions.
   a. With whom did the Lord say the New Covenant will be made (verse 31)?

   b. In verse 32, God tells us that the New Covenant will not be like the older one. What does His description of the older covenant reveal about God's heart?

   c. What New Covenant promises did God make in verse 33?

d. What effects of the New Covenant are foretold in verse 34?

e. From your own knowledge of covenant, what are the most important factors that make this one "new"?

5. Now turn to a similar passage, Jeremiah 32:40. What specific promises did God make here?

6. Next look at Jeremiah 50:4-5.
   a. How is the covenant described in the final lines of this passage?

   b. How does the passage describe the effect of this covenant on the people?

c. How is this different from the general tendency of God's people, as we have seen it so far in our overview of the Old Testament?

7. Now let's listen to more of God's words through the prophet Ezekiel.
   a. What promises did God make to His "flock" in Ezekiel 34:22-31? List them all.

   b. Which of these promises seem especially "new" in comparison with the covenants we saw God make with Abraham, Moses, and David?

8. Turn now to Ezekiel 37:24-28.

   a. What promises did God make here? Again, list them all.

   b. Which of these promises seem especially "new" in comparison with the covenants we saw God make with Abraham, Moses, and David?

9. In Isaiah 55:1-3, God speaks to those are "thirsty" and "who have no money"—with spiritual thirst and spiritual poverty primarily in mind. What promise did God make to them in verse 3?

10. To continue filling in your picture of all the amazing things promised in the New Covenant, reflect on these other passages in Isaiah. Summarize what God promises to His people in each one:
   a. 54:10

   b. 59:21

   c. 61:7-8

11. Now look at the prophecy in Malachi 3:1. The first sentence of the verse refers to the Lord's "messenger." Jesus quoted this verse in reference to John the Baptist (see Matthew 11:10). The rest of Malachi 3:1 deals with someone else.
   a. How is this person described?

   b. Who do you think this passage refers to?

12. Turn now to Isaiah 42:1-7. Here the Lord speaks both *about* and *to* One whom He has both chosen and called.

a. What promises did God make to this chosen One in verse 6?

b. From what you have learned about covenant, what particular significance do you see in this verse? (You may also want to look at Isaiah 49:8.)

This New Covenant foretold by the prophets is the one we find unfolded for us in the New Testament.

13. Look in Luke 1:67-75 at the words spoken about Christ by Zechariah (the father of John the Baptist) before Christ was born. Zechariah spoke these words in the fullness of the Holy Spirit (1:67).

a. What did he say about covenant in this passage?

b. What would the coming of Christ allow God's people to do, according to verses 74-75?

14. Look ahead now to the moment when Jesus helped His disciples (and us) to better understand the meaning of His soon-coming death. Read Luke 22:19-20. Keeping in mind all that you have learned about covenant, explain as fully as possible the significance of Jesus' words here.

15. Scripture gives four titles to Jesus in reference to covenant. Find each one in the passages listed.
    a. Hebrews 9:15

    b. Hebrews 7:22

    c. Malachi 3:1

    d. Isaiah 42:6 (also in 49:8)

Andrew Murray wrote, "All these names point to the one truth: that in the New Covenant, Christ is all in all."[10]

16. In time alone with God, review what you have written down and learned in this lesson. Perhaps you sense something here that God wants you to especially understand and trust Him for at this time. If so, go back and mark it in the lesson, then bring it again before the Lord in prayer and grateful praise. Record here any further thoughts or prayer requests that come to your mind and heart.

A BOND IN BLOOD

A companion Bible study to OUR COVENANT GOD

- Your goals for this lesson are to more deeply understand what God's covenant has accomplished for you, to grasp the seriousness of covenant, and to reflect this increased understanding and awareness in open and honest conversation with God. Ask God to help you accomplish these goals through the powerful teaching of His Holy Spirit at work in your heart and mind.

Covenant…is a walk into death that leads to life.

—Kay Arthur in OUR COVENANT GOD, Chapter 7

What benefit does God's everlasting covenant—and His commitment to it—bring to His people? We receive a multitude of blessings through covenant, but one blessing is the foundation for all the others.

1. Read Psalm 111:9. What foundational blessing for God's people is associated with covenant in this verse?

2. How do you see this same connection reflected in Hebrews 9:15?

3. Study the passage reprinted below, keeping in mind what you studied earlier about the tabernacle. Then,

(a) With one color mark every occurrence of the word *covenant;* (b) with a second color mark every occurrence of the word *blood;* (c) with another, circle every name or pronoun referring to Jesus Christ.

Hebrews 9:11-15

¹¹But when Christ appeared as a high priest of the good things to come, He entered through the greater and more perfect tabernacle, not made with hands, that is to say, not of this creation;

¹²and not through the blood of goats and calves, but through His own blood, He entered the holy place once for all, having obtained eternal redemption.

¹³For if the blood of goats and bulls and the ashes of a heifer sprinkling those who have been defiled sanctify for the cleansing of the flesh,

¹⁴how much more will the blood of Christ, who through the eternal Spirit offered Himself without blemish to God, cleanse your conscience from dead works to serve the living God?

¹⁵And for this reason He is the mediator of a new covenant, in order that since a death has taken place for the redemption of the transgressions that were committed under the first covenant, those who have been called may receive the promise of the eternal inheritance.

a. What is "the greater and more perfect tabernacle" referred to in verse 11? (See Hebrews 9:24 for help on this one.)

b. What did Christ's blood obtain for us, according to verse 12?

c. What does this redemption mean for us in practical terms, according to verse 14?

d. What important points does verse 14 teach us regarding *how* Christ became a sacrifice for our sin?

e. Look at verse 15, which speaks of "this reason." From what you see in the preceding verses, what is this reason?

4. Now look up Hebrews 13:20-21.
   a. How is Christ's blood referred to in this passage?

   b. What did God accomplish through Christ's blood?

c. Look at how God is referred to verse 20. What could be the significance of this in relation to covenant?

d. Now look especially at verse 21. Because of covenant, what does God enable us to do?

e. What for you is the personal significance of this passage at this time in your life?

Let's explore further the crucial significance of *blood* in covenant.

Andrew Murray writes, "The blood is one of the strangest, the deepest, the mightiest, and the most heavenly of the thoughts of God. It lies at the very root of both Covenants, but especially of the New Covenant."[11]

In *The Christ of the Covenants,* O. Palmer Robertson writes, "When God enters into a covenantal relationship with men, he sovereignly institutes a life-and-death bond. A covenant is a bond in blood, or a bond of life and death, sovereignly administered."[12]

Covenant is a bond in *blood.*

5. How are the concepts of *life* and *blood* strongly connected in each of these passages?
   a. Genesis 9:4-6

b. Leviticus 17:11

c. Leviticus 17:14

d. Deuteronomy 12:23

6. A particularly important passage on this topic is John 6:47-58. These are words Jesus spoke to a crowd that had searched for Him after He miraculously fed them. (For the background, see John 6:1-15 and 6:22-27.)

   a. How many times in verses 47-58 does Jesus use the words *life, live,* or *living*?

   b. How many times does He use the words *flesh* or *blood*?

   c. What does Jesus say in this passage about how we can obtain oneness with Him?

d. How did His listeners react to His words, according to verses 52, 60, and 66.

I really believe that in their culture they understood that He was calling them to a oneness through the solemn, binding agreement of covenant, and some didn't want any part of it because of the obligations of covenant.

—Kay Arthur in OUR COVENANT GOD, Chapter 15

e. Now read John 6:67-69. What do you find significant about the way Simon Peter answered Jesus' question?

7. In light of what you have studied so far in this lesson, record here a prayer that accurately reflects your heart's attitude toward your Savior Jesus Christ.

8. Do you remember the story of Cain and Abel and their offerings to God? Review it once again in Genesis 4.

   a. Which of the offerings—Cain's or Abel's—would have involved the shedding of blood?

   b. Which of the offerings was pleasing to God?

   c. After Cain killed his brother in anger, what did God say to him in verse 10?

   d. How does this demonstrate the power of blood?

9. Now look at Hebrews 12:24, which makes a comparison between Abel's blood and Christ's blood.

   a. In what particular way is Christ's blood said to be superior to Abel's?

   b. Because of this fact, what are we told to do in Hebrews 12:25?

10. By sharing in the blood of Christ, we share in one-ness with Him. How do you see this truth reflected in Galatians 2:20?

"I have been crucified with Christ"—there's that walk into death, denying self and taking up the cross....

In covenant you no longer live for yourself; there is a Covenant Partner to consider, and you must be true to that Covenant Partner. Remember, covenant is a bond that commits you to another.

—Kay Arthur in OUR COVENANT GOD, Chapter 7

We find more evidence of the seriousness of covenant as a "walk into death" in the New Testament's teaching on the Lord's Supper (communion).

11. Turn to 1 Corinthians 11.

   a. In verses 20-22, what specific problem did Paul address in how the Lord's Supper was practiced in the Corinthian church?

   b. What are the most important truths he reminded them of in verses 23-26?

c. How many times do you see the word *blood* in verses 25-27?

d. What conclusions did Paul make in verses 27-29?

e. How would you express the teaching of verses 27-29 in your own words, as it applies to believers today?

f. What negative effect of their wrongdoing were the Corinthians experiencing, according to verse 30? (For help in properly interpreting the phrase "fallen asleep," look at 1 Corinthians 15:18-20 and 1 Thessalonians 4:13-15.)

g. What reason for this did Paul give in verse 32?

h. What corrective response does Paul teach in verse 31, and how would you explain what he means?

i. Why does God view the ceremony of the Lord's Supper so seriously? Express your answer in the context of what you have learned about covenant.

If you think you can break the New Covenant, beloved, and go unjudged, you are wrong. Remember what God did when the children of Israel broke the Old Covenant. Can we do the same and escape His judgment? The Sovereign Administrator still watches over covenants.

—Kay Arthur in OUR COVENANT GOD, Chapter 19

---

12. By now you have surely expanded your understanding of what God's covenant relationship with you really means.

a. How would you summarize God's covenant commitments to you?

b. How would you summarize your own covenant obligations to God?

c. Talk about both these perspectives now in a written prayer of praise and commitment to God.

THE LORD WATCH BETWEEN US

A companion Bible study to OUR COVENANT GOD

- Your goal in Lesson 6 is to gain a thorough understanding of the covenant between Jonathan and
  David and to apply its rich lessons to your own life.

When two people enter into covenant, neither
belongs to himself any longer.... In covenant two
become one, and they make an obligation that literally would require their lives if they broke it.

—Kay Arthur in OUR COVENANT GOD, Chapter 7

The man-to-man covenant that Jonathan initiated
with David was to be a crucial factor in the lives of both
these brave warriors. We want to learn from the deeply
symbolic way in which Jonathan undertook this covenant
and from the noble faithfulness with which both these
men upheld their bond to one another.

1. After David had slain Goliath, Israel's King Saul
   was understandably impressed and asked the
   young man to reside in his presence. As a result,
   David and Jonathan, Saul's son, came to know one
   another well.
   a. Read 1 Samuel 18:1-2. Here we find the basis
      of Jonathan's covenant friendship with David.
      What was it?

b. In verse 3, what did Jonathan do and for what reason?

c. List the possessions Jonathan gave to David in verse 4.

Jonathan's actions symbolized his giving of himself to David. We will look more closely at this later. Meanwhile, let's follow the story of these two men to witness what their covenant friendship accomplished.

(For background on the conflict between David and Saul, you may want to look over 1 Samuel 15–16 and 18–19. For background on Jonathan and David's exploits as warriors, refer to 1 Samuel 14 and 17.)

2. In time, David encountered such danger from Saul that he had to flee for his life. In 1 Samuel 20:1, to whom did David go for help?

3. Follow the intense exchange between these two men in 1 Samuel 20. Try to put yourself in their place.
   a. What were David's concerns as expressed in verses 1-3?

b. What cove nant commitment did Jonathan make to David in verse 4?

c. After proposing a plan (verses 5-7) to bring out Saul's true intentions, David made two covenant requests of Jonathan in verse 8. What were they?

d. From what you have studied so far about covenant, were both of these requests within the bounds of appropriate covenant expectations?

e. Who was the third party to their covenant, according to what David said in this verse?

f. How did Jonathan affirm his covenant loyalty in verse 9?

g. In verses 10-13 Jonathan agreed to and extended the plan that David had proposed. Then in verses 14-15 he in turn made two covenant requests of David. What were they?

h. Think about these requests that Jonathan made. What thoughts and assumptions about his future might have been on Jonathan's mind at this point?

4. Now look at 1 Samuel 20:16, where we again see Jonathan initiating a covenant.
   a. With whom was this covenant made?

   b. Why do you think Jonathan wanted to do this?

   c. How would you explain the significance of the statement Jonathan made in this verse?

   d. Likewise, what is the significance of the action Jonathan took in verse 17?

e. Jonathan further refined their plans in verses 18-22. Observe his concluding statement in verse 23. What would these two men understand to be the meaning of such a statement?

5. In the remaining verses of 1 Samuel 20 we see the result of the test that Jonathan and David had devised. Now both men understood Saul's evil intent toward David.
   a. What did Saul tell Jonathan about David in verse 31?

   b. In verse 32, how did Jonathan live up to his covenant obligation to David?

   c. What was the result of Jonathan's words (verses 33-34)?

d. In accordance with their plan, Jonathan let David know (in verses 35-40) what had happened. What respect did David show to Jonathan in verse 41?

e. What factors do you think would account for the intensity of the two men's sorrow in verse 41?

f. In the circumstances that now faced these men, what is the further significance of each point that Jonathan reiterated to David in verse 42?

David was now on the run, along with a growing force of men that soon numbered about four hundred. Saul, meanwhile, was in active pursuit.

6. Observe the scene recorded in 1 Samuel 22:6-8. What do we learn from Saul's words in verse 8?

7. Turn now to 1 Samuel 23, which records what was probably the last meeting between Jonathan and David.

a. Summarize David's situation as presented in verses 13-15.

b. What happened in verse 16?

c. Look at each phrase of Jonathan's as recorded in verse 17. How might each one of these phrases bring encouragement to David?

d. What do these words reveal about Jonathan's heart?

e. What do you think might have been David and Jonathan's reasons for their action recorded in verse 18?

f. Before whom was this action taken?

In a series of dramatic events, the remaining chapters of 1 Samuel record David's continued search for refuge, as well as the deaths of Saul and Jonathan in a battle between Israel and the Philistines on Mount Gilboa. The book of 2 Samuel opens with David discovering this tragic news.

8. Read David's lament for Saul and Jonathan in 2 Samuel 1:17-27.
   a. How did David refer to these men in verses 19, 25, and 27?

b. In verse 26, look at David's praise for the depth of Jonathan's devotion. How would you evaluate the consistency of this statement with what you observed in Jonathan's previous actions toward David?

9. How would you evaluate David's view of the friendship between these two men...
   a. in terms of the benefits it provided for David?

   b. in terms of David's obligations to Jonathan?

10. In light of Jonathan's covenant commitment to David, how do you think the rest of David's life might have been different if his covenant friend had continued living?

11. David's covenant obligations did not end with Jonathan's death. Look back again at 1 Samuel 20:15. On whose behalf did Jonathan request David's committed favor?

12. Let's observe David's loyalty to this commitment.
    a. Summarize the situation described in 2 Samuel 4:4.

    b. Now turn to 2 Samuel 9. In verse 1, what is David's expressed intention?

    c. What important facts did David learn in verses 2-4?

d. What was David's response in verse 5?

13. Study carefully the words spoken by both David and Mephibosheth in verses 6-11.
    a. What do these verses further reveal about David's intentions?

    b. What do they reveal about Mephibosheth?

    c. How would you summarize Mephibosheth's circumstances as described in verses 12-13?

14. There is even more to this story. Turn to 2 Samuel 21, where we see the forces of two covenants at work—Israel's covenant with the Gibeonites (which you studied earlier) and David's continuing covenant with the family of Jonathan.

a. What is the situation as described in verse 1, and what is the reason for it?

b. Summarize the background information provided in verse 2.

c. Summarize the developments recorded in verses 3-6.

d. How did David demonstrate his continued loyalty to Jonathan in verse 7?

e. What else did David do for Jonathan's sake in verses 12-14?

15. From the story of Jonathan and David's covenant friendship, what do you believe are the most important lessons to learn...

    a. in regard to your own friendships?

    b. in regard to your covenant relationship with God?

THE EXCHANGE OF ROBES

Return now to the first covenant ceremony between Jonathan and David, as recorded in 1 Samuel 18:3-4. The first thing Jonathan gave to David was his robe.

By giving David his robe, what was Jonathan saying? Jonathan was telling David, "You're no longer alone—you have a blood brother, a covenant partner. You have put on me!"

—Kay Arthur in OUR COVENANT GOD, Chapter 10

---

16. In our relationship with God we, too, put on His "robe." What do these verses teach us about this covenant truth?

a. Romans 13:14

b. Galatians 3:27

c. Ephesians 4:24

d. Colossians 3:9-10

Remember that you have put on His robe, the Holy Spirit. As a man Jesus lived by the Holy Spirit, so live the same way, beloved. Walk in His likeness by His Spirit, moment by moment, and you shall not fulfill the lust of the flesh!

—Kay Arthur in OUR COVENANT GOD, Chapter 11

Just as we put on God's "robe," so also God, as our Covenant Partner, has put on ours.

17. Summarize what these verses teach about Christ "putting on" your humanity—and what it means for you in practical terms:
    a. Philippians 2:6-8

    b. Hebrews 2:14

    c. Hebrews 2:17-18

    d. Hebrews 4:15

THE EXCHANGE OF ARMOR

This exchange of armor was also a common practice in cutting covenant. And what did it mean? It was a symbolic way of signifying that one covenant partner was taking on the other partner's enemies.

—Kay Arthur in OUR COVENANT GOD, Chapter 12

---

18. What conclusions can you make from Romans 12:19-21 about God coming to our aid?

19. Turn to Psalm 105.
    a. What covenant truths are affirmed in verses 8-11?

    b. How did God demonstrate His protection of
       His covenant people in verses 12-15?

When you are in covenant with Jesus Christ, beloved,
the whole Godhead is your refuge. The Father, the
Son, and the Holy Spirit in all their omnipotence
become your defenders. Therefore you can leave all
thought of vengeance to God, while you instead
manifest to your enemies the unconditional love of
God.

—Kay Arthur in OUR COVENANT GOD, Chapter 12

Just as God takes on our enemies, so we are to take
on His. And how do we do that?

20. Summarize the covenant truths you find in these
    passages:
    a. John 15:18-19

    b. James 4:4

c. 1 John 2:15-16

21. What truth about God's enemy (and ours) is found in Ephesians 6:12?

THE EXCHANGE OF BELTS

Do you remember when Jonathan gave David...his belt? He was saying, "When you run out of strength, I'll be there. My strength, my ability, are at your disposal in any hour of need. I am your resource."

—Kay Arthur in OUR COVENANT GOD, Chapter 14

---

22. Summarize these assurances of God's strength on behalf of His covenant partners.
a. Nehemiah 8:10

b. 2 Corinthians 12:9-10

c. Ephesians 6:10-11

23. In time alone with God, review what you have written down and learned in this lesson. Record also any further thoughts or prayer requests that come to your mind and heart.

YOUR COVENANT RICHES

A companion Bible study to OUR COVENANT GOD

- Your goal in Lesson 7 is to explore various biblical truths through the fresh perspective of all that you have learned about covenant and to see these truths illustrated in a variety of additional customs from mankind's covenant heritage.

COVENANT WOUNDS AND SCARS

For covenant partners the scar [resulting from a covenant cut] served as a constant reminder of their promise. After making incisions in their wrists, the two parties would rub their wounds with something that would irritate the flesh and leave a scar. Sometimes it would be the dirt of the earth. In later times it might be gunpowder.

Whatever the abrasive, it had the sole purpose of leaving a scar—a brand-mark that would remind them, every time they raised their hand, that they were in covenant with another. If the cut was in the wrist or palm, then every movement of the hand—dressing, eating, working—would bring to mind one's covenant partner and one's commitment and obligation to care for him forever.

—Kay Arthur in OUR COVENANT GOD, Chapter 16

---

1. What do we learn about our Lord's wounds in these passages?
   a. Isaiah 53:5

   b. John 20:25-27

   c. Revelation 5:6

2. What does God say about His people in Isaiah 49:16?

The One who has chosen you now lifts up His hands. In the name of His wounds He claims the right to be not only your Savior but also your Lord, your Leader, your Master, your God.

—Kay Arthur in OUR COVENANT GOD, Chapter 16

---

3. How did the apostle Paul describe his scars in Galatians 6:17?

Having mingled blood, the covenant partners would then share "the blessings of covenant." Since two had become one, they now would have all things in common. One by one they would give an account of their possessions and their debts. The covenant partner had a right—and an obligation—to be aware of every detail.

When we come to the end of our resources, our Covenant Partner is there to meet our needs. Recognizing this brings full understanding of the promise, "And my God shall supply all your needs according to His riches in glory in Christ Jesus."

—Kay Arthur in OUR COVENANT GOD, Chapter 18

4. How do these passages indicate the wealth of your covenant relationship with God?
   a. Psalm 23:1

   b. Romans 8:32

   c. 1 Corinthians 1:30

   d. 1 Corinthians 3:21-23

e. 2 Corinthians 9:8

f. Ephesians 1:3

g. Ephesians 1:7

h. Luke 15:31

5. In what ways are we to share all that we "possess" with God, our Covenant Partner?
   a. Luke 14:33

   b. Acts 2:44-45

   c. Acts 4:32

d. Philippians 3:7-8

THE EXCHANGE OF NAMES

Often in covenant, after the sharing of blessings
there was a changing of names.... The exchanging
of names, or adopting part of their covenant partner's name, testified to the oneness of covenant!
— Kay Arthur in OUR COVENANT GOD, Chapter 18

---

6. In what way do you bear your Covenant Partner's
name?
a. Matthew 18:20

b. 1 Peter 4:16

c. Revelation 2:17

7. How does Mark 10:45 show your Covenant Partner sharing your name?

Another name we share as God's covenant partners is that of "friend." As Kay Arthur writes, *"Friend* is a covenant term."

8. Record how these verses establish the title "friend" for God's covenant partner Abraham.
   a. 2 Chronicles 20:7

   b. Isaiah 41:8

   c. James 2:23

9. How did God demonstrate His friendship with Abraham in Genesis 18:17-19?

10. Read the words Jesus spoke in John 15:12-16.
    a. In verse 15, what reason does Jesus give for calling His followers "friends"?

b. What other covenant truths do you find in this passage?

THE COVENANT MEAL

The exchanging of names would often be followed by a covenant meal. Like the other covenant customs, this one also has been seen throughout man's cultural history....

In the covenant meal, the total oneness of covenant, the insoluble bond was once again emphasized as they placed a piece of bread in their covenant partner's mouth and said, "You are eating me." Then would come the cup of covenant, a cup oftentimes holding a drop of each person's blood. Offering it to his partner, each would say, "You are drinking me."

—Kay Arthur in OUR COVENANT GOD, Chapter 18

---

11. Summarize the covenant significance of these passages:
    a. Isaiah 25:6

b. Matthew 8:11

c. Matthew 22:1-14

d. Revelation 19:9

MARRIAGE

Marriage is itself a covenant, and even today our wedding ceremonies are filled with covenant imagery.
12. In Malachi 2:13-16, God speaks to His people against divorce.
   a. In verse 14, what terms are used to describe a man's wife?

   b. What commands are repeated in verses 15 and 16?

   c. How does this passage reinforce the essential meaning of covenant (even outside marriage)?

13. How is marriage a picture of the Lord's relationship with us, according to these passages?
    a. Ephesians 5:25-32

    b. Revelation 19:6-8

14. In time alone with God, review what you have written down and learned in this lesson. Record also any further thoughts or prayer requests that come to your mind and heart.

THREE SALVATION COVENANTS

A companion Bible study to OUR COVENANT GOD

- Your goals in this final lesson are to understand how the three major covenants in Scripture relate together and to grasp their significance to your own salvation and life. Ask God to help you accomplish these goals through the powerful teaching of His Holy Spirit at work in your heart and mind.

Not understanding how the covenants play into our salvation can bring a great deal of confusion and bondage. It's happening within our churches today.

—Kay Arthur in OUR COVENANT GOD, Chapter 22

THE ABRAHAMIC COVENANT

1. Let's focus again on what God promised Abraham.
   a. In Genesis 12:1-3 we see God commanding Abram to leave his homeland and follow God to a new country. What did God promise Abram at this time?

b. In Genesis 15 we see the covenant ceremony in which the flaming torch passed through the pieces of the sacrificed animals. What did God promise Abram in verses 5 and 18?

c. Now turn to Genesis 17, where Abram received the name Abraham. What did God promise him in verses 6-8?

d. Genesis 22 tells the story of Abraham obeying God by offering up his son Isaac as a sacrifice. After God provided a substitute sacrifice, what promises did He make to Abraham in verses 17-18?

e. Which of all these promises have a bearing on your life, and in what way?

2. Look at Romans 4:11-12, in which Paul is speaking of Abraham.
   a. According to these verses, of whom is Abraham the father?

   b. What example from Abraham's life are we to follow, according to this passage?

3. Study Romans 4:13-18.
   a. What does this passage tell us about the law?

   b. From what you see in this passage, what is the right response to God's promises?

   c. Who benefits from Abraham's correct response?

4. Look up Galatians 3:6-9 and explain the connection made there between Abraham and New Testament believers.

5. What is the main point Paul teaches in Galatians 3:16? (This verse refers back to the promises mentioned in the passages listed in Question 1. The Hebrew word for "seed" in these passages is usually translated as "descendants" in our Bibles.)

The Law, or Old Covenant

Unlike the other biblical covenants, the law was not a permanent, everlasting covenant.

6. Read Galatians 3:15-18, in which Paul refers both to the law and to God's covenant with Abraham, which was made many centuries before the law was given. According to this passage, did the law nullify God's covenant with Abraham?

7. Now study Galatians 3:19-25. List all the main points Paul makes here about the law.

The Seed was promised through the Abrahamic Covenant. Until the Seed came, the Law was given for the purpose of defining our sin, pointing out sin as sin while also, as we see in this verse [Galatians 3:23], protecting us, keeping us from sin by defining it so we don't reap its awful consequences.

The Law walls us in with its commandments so we don't suffer the dangerous consequences of living outside them.

—Kay Arthur in OUR COVENANT GOD, Chapter 23

---

8. Now look at Galatians 3:24-25. What are the main points made in this passage?

The Law serves as our tutor. Through it we gain both the knowledge of what we need to do *and* the realization that we can't do it in our own strength. And this, beloved, is what brings us to faith in Christ Jesus. Through our tutor we learn to desire the righteousness of the Law and we realize that we can't get it on our own; it comes only through faith.

After our "tutor" has done its work, we come to the place where we throw up our hands in surrender and say, "I can't achieve righteousness. I'm a sinner, a transgressor of the Law; there's no hope!" And we hear Jesus say, *"I* can. Will you believe Me and let Me in?"

When we believe, we throw open the door so our Lord and Savior—Jesus Christ, the Seed of Abraham, the Mediator of the New Covenant—may graciously enter in.

And then God looks at you and says, "Justified" —declared righteous by faith. For He sees "Christ in you, the hope of glory!"

—Kay Arthur in OUR COVENANT GOD, Chapter 23

THE NEW COVENANT

9. Look at Hebrews 8:7-13. This passage quotes from Jeremiah's New Covenant prophecy in Jeremiah 31, which we studied in Lesson 4. In Hebrews, the verses that precede and follow the quotation compare the New Covenant with the Old.

a. What comparison of the two covenants is made in verses 7-8?

b. What comparison is made in verse 13?

10. Chapters 9 and 10 in Hebrews continue to explore how the New Covenant—the covenant made through the blood of Christ—is superior to the Old. Summarize how this superiority is presented in each of these passages in Hebrews:
a. 9:11-12

b. 9:13-15

c. 9:23-26

d. 10:1-10

e. 10:11-18

11. Look at Hebrews 10:19-22.
    a. What blessings are ours because of the New
        Covenant?

    b. And how did we obtain these blessings, accord-
        ing to this passage?

Here is the jewel you are to treasure in days of
doubt or anxiety: Our Covenant God has come
down and honored us in all our weakness, all our
infirmities. He honored us even though we sinned
against Him. It was while we were helpless, while
we were without hope—while we were sinners, enemies of God—that God sought us out to cut a
covenant on our behalf!

—Kay Arthur in OUR COVENANT GOD, Chapter 5

12. On the basis of this superiority of the New
Covenant and the blood of Christ, the author of
Hebrews presents commands from God for us to
follow.

a. List the commands given in Hebrews 10:22-25.

b. Which of these commands do you believe is
most important for you to focus on at this time
in your life?

c. What can you do to more diligently obey this
command?

13. Look at how the New Covenant was announced in Luke 22:20. Imagine that you were present on the night when Jesus said this and that the Old Testament prophecies of the New Covenant were fixed in your memory. What thoughts might go through your mind as Jesus spoke these words?

14. Revelation 13:8 describes Jesus as "the Lamb slain from the foundation of the world" (KJV). Because of this sacrifice, planned and accomplished in eternity, what has been eternally true about us, according to Ephesians 1:4?

Oh, beloved, do you realize that since the advent of time, before the creation of man, the New Covenant was in the heart and mind of our omniscient God? In an eternal council the Holy Three sat before the crystal sea and laid out their plan of redemption. The Messenger of the New Covenant would come. The covenant sacrifice, the Lamb of God, would be slain. The promise of the Spirit would be given, and man would become one with his God.

The New Covenant has always been in the heart and plan of the Father, the Son, and the Spirit. But it would happen in God's time, in His order. Other covenants must come first, all in preparation for the ultimate covenant, the covenant that would accomplish what the others could not: holiness of life by the power of the indwelling Spirit.

—Kay Arthur in OUR COVENANT GOD, Chapter 24

15. Look again at Hebrews 8:10. What exactly does God promise to do for His people?

16. Romans 8:1-11 teaches us how this promise is fulfilled in our lives. In light of what you now know about covenant, how would you explain the teaching of this passage?

We are not left to fend for ourselves. We now have a
Covenant Partner. With the New Covenant comes
the promise of the indwelling Helper....

The gift of the Spirit sets us free from the princi-
ple of sin and death which reigned in our bodies.
Now we are able to walk according to the Spirit; we
have our Covenant Partner's strength....

The gift of the Holy Spirit given under the New
Covenant is the guarantee of our inheritance, our
sharing in covenant oneness all that belongs to our
Covenant God and Savior.

—Kay Arthur in OUR COVENANT GOD, Chapter 24

17. Turn now to 2 Corinthians 3:4-6.
    a. What is the "confidence" that Paul wrote about
       here?

    b. The word "letter" in verse 6 refers to the Old
       Covenant, which was written on tablets of
       stone. (Notice the reference to these in verse 3.)
       What difference did Paul point out between the
       "letter" and the Holy Spirit?

    c. What impact should this difference have on how
       you live out the New Covenant day by day?

The Old Covenant exposed our sin and our need. The New Covenant provides the solution: the Holy Spirit.

The Old Covenant enlightened. The New Covenant empowers.

The Old Covenant revealed our sin. The New Covenant releases us from sin's power.

—Kay Arthur in OUR COVENANT GOD, Chapter 24

WITH ALL YOUR HEART

18. What promises concerning the hearts of God's people are made in these Old Testament passages?
   a. Deuteronomy 30:6

   b. Jeremiah 24:7

   c. Jeremiah 32:40

19. What promise concerning our hearts does Jesus make in Matthew 5:8?

20. What are we commanded to do with our hearts in Matthew 22:37?

Only through the New Covenant are we able to fulfill this command and to know the blessing of a pure heart that Jesus pronounced in His Sermon on the Mount.

21. What do these passages teach about our New Covenant hearts?
    a. Romans 10:9-10

    b. Ephesians 1:18

    c. 1 Timothy 1:5

    d. 2 Timothy 2:22

    e. 1 Peter 1:22

22. Take time to review each of the previous lessons in this study guide.
    a. Restate here (in summary form) the most important truths about covenant and our Covenant God that you have studied in this book.

    b. How would you express what you believe are the most important changes God wants to see in your life as a result of your study of covenant?

You have seen how the Scriptures are saturated with the concept of covenant and how understanding covenant is the doorway to a deeper understanding of all that God has so graciously revealed to us in His Word. You are now equipped, beloved, to know and to do His Word as never before. Therefore I must tell you that the only way to continue deepening your trust and understanding of God is to continue studying and meditating on His entire Word, in reliance on the work and teaching of His Holy Spirit. Remember that God's ways are not our ways, His thoughts are not ours.

With all my heart I commend you for completing this journey of exploring God's covenant thoughts and covenant ways, that in this hurting and hurtful world you may truly "go out with joy, and be led forth with peace."

—Kay Arthur in OUR COVENANT GOD, Chapter 24

NOTES

1. H. Clay Trumbull, *The Blood Covenant* (1885; reprint, Kirkwood, Mo.: Impact Christian Books, 1975), pages 4, 57.

2. Lawrence O. Richards, *Expository Dictionary of Bible Words* (Grand Rapids: Zondervan, 1985, 1991), page 193-194.

3. James Strong, "Hebrew and Chaldee Dictionary," *Exhaustive Concordance of the Bible* (Nashville: Holman Bible Publishers), page 24, #1285.

4. Elmer Smick, "Covenant," *Theological Wordbook of the Old Testament,* vol. I, ed. R. Laird Harris, Gleason L. Archer, and Bruce Waltke (Chicago: Moody Press, 1980), page 128, #282a.

5. Louis Berkhof, *Systematic Theology* (Grand Rapids: Eerdmans, 1941), page 262.

6. W.E. Vine, *An Expository Dictionary of Biblical Words* (Nashville: Thomas Nelson, 1985).

7. Strong, page 22, #1242.

8. Richards, page 195.

9. Andrew Murray, *The Two Covenants* (originally published in 1898; Christian Literature Crusade edition: 1974, Fort Washington, Pennsylvania), page 51.

10. Murray, page 86.

11. Murray, page 76.

12. O. Palmer Robertson, *The Christ of the Covenants* (Phillipsburg, New Jersey: Presbyterian and Reformed Publishing, 1980), page 4.